DRESSER DOLLS
and
OTHER CHINA FIGURALS

by

Frieda Marion and Norma Werner

The current values in this book should be used only as a guide. They are not intended to set prices, which vary from one section of the country to another. Auction prices as well as dealer prices vary greatly and are affected by condition as well as demand. Neither the Author nor the Publisher assumes responsibility for any losses that might be incurred as a result of consulting this guide.

Additional copies of this book may be ordered from:

COLLECTOR BOOKS
P.O. Box 3009
Paducah, Kentucky 42001

@$7.95 Add $1.00 for postage and handling.

Copyright: Frieda Marion, Norma Werner, 1983
ISBN: 0-89145-223-0

TO
ELLEN MARISE TITUS
and
HELEN AUDIER

ACKNOWLEDGEMENTS

Much of the material here was collected while the authors were doing research on the *Collector's Encyclopedia of Half-Dolls* (Collector Books, 1979), and we are greatly indebted to all those persons who made contributions to that work and whose names are listed therein. Collectors whose Dresser Dolls and other treasures are shown here are mentioned in the illustration captions and listed in the index.

It is, alas, impossible to recount everyone who has in some way influenced the production of this book, but we are grateful and thank you all.

Frieda Marion, Norma Werner, 1982

Research by both authors. Photos by Norma Werner unless otherwise specified. Text by Frieda Marion.

PRICE GUIDE

During the time it's manufactured, a product is priced by computing costs of material, labor, overhead, advertising and distribution. Antiques and collectibles can't be priced this way. Records of production are seldom available and there can never be information on the number of identical items which have survived damage or destruction.

Items shown here were made on a very different economy. Today's values reflect the collector's tastes, not production costs. For instance, any china figure bearing a tray with teapot and cups will command a high price because the half-doll model representing *La Belle Chocolatiere*, the Walter Baker trademark, is still the top-drawing design among half-figures. Models in the Dressel and Kister Medieval Series are close runners-up, and collectors always pay more for an article which can be identified by maker and country or origin.

Of course good design and quality workmanship are sought in Dresser Dolls as in any field. Condition should also be taken into account. Connoisseurs have traditionally considered that damage to a porcelain piece brings down its value.

As far as possible, our price guide reflects actual sales within recent months. However, many items were obtained by the owners in years past, and often there is only one example of a model shown to us today, so in some cases we've had to use current values for similar articles.

TABLE OF CONTENTS

Page

Chapter One
What are Dresser Dolls?

The appeal of little china figures has existed ever since the first primitive artist poked and patted a handful of clay into something resembling a living creature. Human beings in miniature were subjects for the modeler long before the secret of making real porcelain reached the Western world, but only within the past three hundred years has mastery of this medium enabled us to produce the amazingly detailed china figures possible by casting and firing in hard-paste porcelain.

The charming, light-hearted and relatively inexpensive objects we discuss in this book represent a period from the latter part of the 19th to the early half of the 20th centuries when porcelain was no longer a rarity and the craze for decorative china figures had reached the mass market.

Despite the popularity of shelf-pieces, buying purely ornamental figurines was viewed by most working people as somewhat of an extravagance if not actually sinful, but a china figure that was useful as well as pretty was bound to have sales potential. Decoration had often been added to household artifacts, now a natural development was to make the figurines into utilitarian objects. How about boxes?

Boxes or small containers are surely a necessity in every home, and an endless variety of figures could be modeled to become containers. Cast in porcelain they would neither break nor chip as easily as earthenware. Creating the effect of elegance, they had practical uses which would soothe the conscience of the most thrifty householder.

There were many uses for china boxes modeled in the shape of lovely ladies or little children, with their flaring skirts forming containers and their upper bodies making the lids.

"Such a pretty jar, and see . . . she lifts right off at the first ruffle and you can keep your talcum there in the skirt! Just like a little Dresden statue but so useful! Isn't it clever?"

Tiny figures concealed thimbles and rings, while large china boxes hid sewing aids, talcum powder or assorted trinkets. Ideas expanded. Reclining figures were designed as small dishes to hold pins, powder-puffs or soap. Lamp bases were modeled and cast in the shape of romantic ladies and gentlemen similar to the early Meissen groups.

Well into the 20th century all manner of china figures combining the serviceable with the ornamental might be found in average homes. Usually they were found on what magazine writers of the day called Milady's Dressing Table.

The name "Dresser Dolls" derives from the fact that so many of these pretty porcelain figurals were accoutrements of the dressing table. China powder-boxes, pintrays, cologne bottles and small lamps were all placed on dressing tables or bureaus for display and easy access. The word **doll** refers to much more than a plaything, and certainly dresser dolls weren't given to small children, although we know that they delighted children as well as adults. The dresser dolls of which we write are china items modeled to represent living creatures and they were designed to be in some way serviceable as well as ornamental.

Photo by Norma Werner from her collection

A typical Lovely Lady powder-box, 7¼" high. In this example, the bodice, overskirt and roses are painted yellow. Similar designs have been found in papier-mache labeled "TERRE DE RETZ/Made in France" but this porcelain box is unmarked.

$50.00-100.00

7

Photo by Norma Werner from her collection

Porcelain lamp base incised with the entwined "GH" symbol of Karl Schneiders Erben; also "DEP/17441/GERMANY."

$50.00-100.00

8

Collection of Eleanor Lar Rieu   *Photo by James Lar Rieu*

Impressed "3638 Bavaria" on the bottom of the box, this same model has been found without the Art Deco flowers painted on the skirt.

$100.00-150.00

9

Photo by Norma Werner from her collection

A curtseying dame in a fine dress trimmed with "pin lace" enameling, incised inside the top "6 III," with the hand-painted numerals "14" inside both lid and base.

$50.00-100.00

Collection of Norma Werner

Here we have a mingling of 18th Century and Art Deco which can only be described by the German word "Kitsch."

Black trim on the purple bodice and panniers contrasts with the yellow pleated skirt, while the forward thrust of the lady's leg and her eye-catching red slipper belie her demure expression.

It's very likely that this lamp is part of a set in which a similar model was fashioned as a powder-box.

Up to $50.00

Collection of Wilma Jo Saylor
Photo by Dern Studio

This very fine porcelain Dresser Doll would make a lovely shelf decoration with never a hint that her flounced skirt was hiding a lady's jewels. Apparently she was destined for another career, however, as she's marked "Colonial Powder Box." She also has a faint manufacturer's mark in the form of a shield, and the word "Bavaria."

$150.00-200.00

11

Collection of Norma Werner

A striking Dresser Doll, 5" high, bearing the incised mark of the maker, H. Mercier. The rest of the inscription, "Paradis/Paris/Made in France/700", is hand-painted in red.

$50.00-100.00

12

Collection of Mary Griffith   Photo by Norma Werner

We may safely assume that china pieces marked "Foreign" were meant for export, but as several countries used this designation, it really isn't much help to us in determining the origin of this powder box.

This classic Old-Fashioned Girl model is 6" high.

$50.00-100.00

13

Photo by Norma Werner from her collection

A typical powder-box of the early 20th century, the wide skirt makes a roomy receptacle and the little torso becomes the lid. Decorated in pink, cream and blue, she makes a charming dressing table ornament.

Up to $50.00

Collection of Joyce Mineart
Photo by Norma Werner

The basic design for a figural powder-box was an Old-Fashioned Girl. The flared skirt made a roomy receptacle and the torso fitted neatly as a lid. This lady, with her parasol and draped shawl, is incised "Germany 14791" and bears the Karl Schneider trademark.
$100.00-150.00

Collection of Wilma Jo Saylor
Photo by Dern Studio

This charming box representing a young woman with a muff is 7¼" high and made of heavy bisque, unmarked.

A similar model over 8" high is shown in Antiques, Octopus Books, London 1978, illustrating the feature "Old Tobacco Jars" by Roger Fresco-Corbu who states that it is French biscuit ware by Gille, jeune of Paris and dates about 1885.
$200.00-250.00

Collection of Patricia Conn
Photo by Ralph A. Meranto, Jr.

Dresser Dolls were not playthings, but this gold-trimmed china box might have been given to a very young lady for her special treasures.
Up to $50.00

Photo by Norma Werner from her collection

Heavy porcelain powder-box, stamped "MADE IN ENGLAND" as shown, with the following hand-painted marks on the bottom - "3 A 166".

$50.00-100.00

16

Germany
3389

Collection of Joyce Mineart   Photo by Norma Werner

   Incised "Germany/3389," this pensive young woman is seated in a gold-trimmed chair, strumming her lute.
   A very decorative powder or trinket box.

$100.00-150.00

Collection of Norma Werner

Three pieces of a dresser set stamped "Bavaria." The cologne bottle stoppers have cork inserts with glass daubers. The figural powder-box lid is identical to the stopper tops. Bottles are 7"; powder-box 5". $50.00-100.00 set

Collection of Florence Eikelberner   *Photo by Norma Werner*

The small dish for face powder is shaped to represent the young lady's shoulders, and her china head, attached to a powder-puff, sets inside. There is a problem of proportion, however, and as the powder diminishes the head sinks lower and lower until her fluffy boa disappears into the dish and the lady assumes a hunched and dejected appearance.

The powder dish is incised "MADE IN GERMANY/74153."

$50.00-100.00

Chapter Two
Powder and Trinket Boxes

There is another reason to label our subject Dresser Dolls, and it is because at least one manufacturer used the term and stamped it on his product.

Many models of china boxes are clearly marked "Madame Pompadour/Dresser Dolls/Germany." These dresser dolls are usually designed to represent dainty young ladies whose wide, ruffled skirts form bowls for powder or trinkets.

Vanity Boxes was another name used in catalog listings, and since in the 1920's a dressing table was also called a vanity table, there is logic in this term, too. Not all dresser dolls or vanity boxes were modeled like the Madame Pompadour full-length figures. Many were made with the figure attached to the lid in a sitting, standing or kneeling position, and great ingenuity was shown by the designers who made the jars beneath to resemble large cushions, wicker chairs, or curved-back love seats.

Besides the maker of the Madame Pompadour dresser dolls, there were other manufacturers who stamped or incised their work. In his *Handbuch des Europaischen Porzellans*, (Munich, 1974), Ludwig Danckert mentions "Luxusporzellan" or luxury porcelains as being included in the output of many late-19th century factories, suggesting that they made fancy china pieces as well as table-ware.

W. Goebel Porzellanfabrik, Oeslau, West Germany, made a fair share of these novelties, incising them with the crown and entwined initials familiar to collectors of Goebel half-dolls and Hummel figurines. Carl Schneider's mark is also seen on dresser dolls, and so is the crown and slashed S of the Voigt company of Sitzendorf.

Were dresser dolls and their relations . . . cologne bottles, pin trays, figural lamps and such . . . made only in Germany? Of course not. Japan had a tremendous output of these china items, much of which came onto the market as reproductions or imitations of the German ware when World War I hindered exportation from that country. Dresser dolls were made in France and in England, too, although apparently not in such quantity as came from Bavaria, and a few dresser dolls were even made here in the United States.

Darlene Hurst Dommel, writing about Fulper and Stangl pottery in the April 1975 issue of the *National Antiques Review*, mentions how, when World War I curtailed the supply of imported heads, Fulper Brothers in Fleming, New Jersey, made doll heads of bisque. She goes on to say that "the same bisque was used in limited production of other artware, including figural lamps and covered powder boxes." Her article is illustrated with a photo of a bisque figural lamp in the shape of a seated young lady, with the area beneath her wide-spread skirt fitted with an electrical attachment and light bulb, an item bearing the Fulper trademark as proof that some dresser dolls were made in this country.

Wherever possible throughout this book we have indicated the maker of the article in the illustration captions, and we give examples of trademarks and inscriptions so that readers can become familiar with the work and marks of various factories.

Writing about the early 20th century, Don Klein says in his *All Color Book of Art Deco*, that "Figures of ladies were immensely popular" (during this period) "and most of the famous porcelain manufacturers had some in their catalogue." We think this can be said of the dresser dolls. It seems very likely that most of the successful porcelain factories of the early 20th century experimented with some line of china figurals that could have claim, however far-fetched, to being useful, and that the manufacturers marketed these novelty pieces along with their purely ornamental figures.

Collection of Norma Werner

A shallow powder-box with the lid removed. A typical Dresser Doll, with an unidentified incised mark as shown.

Up to $50.00

20

Collection of Norma Werner

A 4½" high unmarked powder-box designed to represent an 18th Century lady carrying her reticule.

Up to $50.00

Photo by Norma Werner from her own collection

There is a charming, ageless quality in the fanciful costume of wide-brimmed hat and petal-flounced skirt of this 4½" high trinket-box.

Up to $50.00

21

Collection of Eleanor Lar Rieu
Photo by James Lar Rieu

This powder-box by the W. Goebel Porzellan-fabrik is modeled to depict a young lady in bathing costume seated on a wicker chair apparently draped with a large bath towel. Collector Chris Iwanski has a similar model with a stoppered opening for cologne, suggesting that there may have been a number of various pieces of this design making a dressing table set.

$100.00-150.00

Collection of Frieda Marion

A papyrus blossom decorates this delightful green dresser jar. Is the young maiden on the lid the Biblical Miriam, partially submerged in the river but keeping a protective watch on her baby brother Moses?

Up to $50.00

Collection of Joyce Mineart   Photo by Norma Werner

Marked "Aladin/Made in France/L.R." The two-piece jar has an opening in the lid for the half-figure fastened onto the powder-puff.

To use the puff, the lid must first be removed by sliding it up over the figure, a finicky maneuver lest the lady be chipped in the process.

$100.00-150.00

Photo by Norma Werner from her collection

All are marked "Madame Pompadour/Dresser Dolls/Germany" with either the addition of the word "ERPHILA" or the initials "E & R."

$50.00-100.00 each

23

Collection of Norma Werner

Dressed in a frock of royal blue and bright yellow, this Flapper Dresser Doll of the late 1920's is 5½" high. When the lid is lifted the lower three ruffles and the lady's legs are disclosed as the container of face powder and a large, flat puff.

Collectors have found a variety of similar powder-boxes marked "D.R.G.M." with a 4 digit number beginning with 5, all of which appear to have the same maker.

$50.00-100.00

Collection of Maxine Burkholder

One of two Dresser Dolls so similar in design that it's probable they were part of a set. The 4½" powder-box has a wreath of applied flowers around the lid, missing from the 5½" trinket-box which has painted flowers above the skirt ruffle. The torsos are obviously from the same basic model.

$50.00-100.00

Pierrette is a china half-doll fastened to a swansdown powder-puff sitting in the shallow dish held aloft by Pierrot. This ingenious design, decorated in black and white, reflects the early 20th Century popularity of the Italian Comedy motif.

$200.00-250.00

An oval vanity box with a pleading Pierrot kneeling on the lid. "Bavaria" in gold is stamped on the bottom of the box.

$100.00-150.00

Collection of Mary Griffith
Photo by Norma Werner

Of pale pink frosted or satin glass, this 8¼"
powder-box was designed in the Art Deco
period with a contemporary short skirt. The
lady's legs form a pedestal supporting the
powder container, in this model a somewhat
awkward device.

Up to $50.00

Here the powder container is the lower half
of the lady's skirt with her legs modeled to form
the stem or column holding it aloft. The lid em-
compasses the top part of her bouffant skirt
which is painted tomato red.

$100.00-150.00

26

Photo by Norma Werner from her collection

This 6" trinket-box is stamped in red as follows: "Madame Pompadour/Dresser Doll/ERPHILA/Germany." The manufacturers attempted to please all tastes and this blonde lovely is gowned in bright lime-green.

$50.00-100.00

Collection of Bern Brekas
Photo by Tony Brekas

Depicting a little girl with a great big bow, this 5½" trinket-box made a popular gift in the 1920's.

Up to $50.00

3855
Germany

Collection of Joyce Mineart   Photo by Norma Werner

   The upper portion of this pretty dancer forms the lid of a powder-box, while her legs and
the round cushion on which she is seated are modeled to make the container.

$50.00-100.00

28

Collection of Eleanor Lar Rieu   Photo by James Lar Rieu

This butterfly decorated powder-box is incised with the mark of the Voigt factory, Sitzendorf.
$50.00-100.00

29

Heubach is a name collectors associate with play dolls as well as small statues, "piano babies" and other porcelain novelties. This 8½" bisque trinket box is easily recognized as a Heubach infant with modeled dimples and intaglio painted eyes, and for further corroboration there is the incised Heubach trademark on the back.

A purely ornamental piano baby was also produced in this same delightful design.

$150.00-200.00

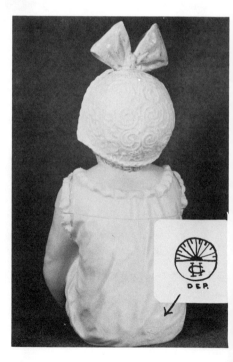

Chapter Three
Figural Lamps

Naturally the shining lights among dresser dolls are the boudoir lamps. Not that the average woman in the 1920s actually had a *boudoir* in which to use them, but she may have had a dressing table and she certainly had a bureau or chest of drawers on which to place a small lamp.

The word "boudoir" was a popular euphonism at a time when anything of French derivation was considered elegant and desirable, although in most families there seldom was space enough to set aside a room just for a lady's private use. More likely, a married woman shared the front bedroom with her husband, and a young girl occupied sleeping quarters along with one or two sisters.

Still, women's magazines glossed over this fact and published numerous articles telling the ladies how to make dainty items to decorate their boudoirs. All over America bedrooms were embellished with hand-embroidered, lace-trimmed pillows and doilies, and thousands of American husbands slept in rooms which, if not exact replicas of French noblewomen's boudoirs, were as close as their wives' talents and the family budget could achieve.

When houses were wired for electricity and the old gas mantles were blown out for the last time, the fashionable little boudoir lamps took over upstairs. The basic design for these bedroom lights seems to have loosely copied Dresden or Meissen figures, but were topped off with electrical fixtures and fancy lamp shades. Old-fashioned girls with hoop skirts were as popular in lamp designs as among dresser-boxes.

Porcelain ruffles, fans, nosegays and musical instruments abound, and there are many pairs of figures costumed in wonderous clothes inspired by a very superficial concept of 18th century French court dress.

A copy of the November 1912 issue of *The Modern Priscilla*, that arbiter of what was new and correct for the diligent needlewoman, repeats the word "French" over and again. It carries ads for French lace, French ostrich feathers, French china and French embroidery. Among suggestions for three dozen different Christmas presents there are mentions of "festoons of dainty French embroidered flowers and leaves" on a tea apron; an "exact copy of a French cup" for china painting; a transfer pattern for "French and Eyelet work" on a chemise; and the "best quality French lawn" for dressmaking.

There is also a full page feature by Ethelyn J. Morris titled "Two Sets of Table Linen in French and Eyelet Design." Clearly anything remotely French stood for beauty, refinement and high fashion. Boudoir lamps were tremendously popular. All that was termed French did not come from France, however.

We know that in New Jersey the Fulper pottery company made some of these little lamps, and are told about them in Anne and John DeMelio's article, "Famous Fulper Ladies," in the July 11, 1979 issue of the *Antique Trader*. Top choice for collectors are the Fulper figural perfume lamps. "A small amount of perfume was poured into the well of the base," Mrs. DeMelio wrote. The mild warmth from the light bulb allowed the fragrance to rise and escape through tiny air holes in the head of the porcelain figure.

Mrs. DeMelio wrote that lamps in her private collection have the Fulper mark in a rectangle, and that some also bear Martin Stangl's "MS" mark as well. Stangl headed the Fulper company in the 1920s, and designed much of the art pottery they produced.

Most of the boudoir lamps were made in Germany or Bavaria by the same companies making figurines, half-dolls and powder-boxes. Nevertheless, they were often advertised as French.

In 1927, Daniel Low and Company issued a gift catalog with a page headed "To Give Your Boudoir Charm," advertising a French Boudoir Light with a base described as a "dainty and demure period lady in all her old-fashioned loveliness." The lamp came with a Georgette shade with gold braid and French flower motif . . . complete with silk cord and socket. The shade was offered in rose, blue or orchid, and the whole thing was advertised as a special at $5.00. Who could resist? We doubt if it was made in France though, as the demure period lady is the same model we've seen produced on a powder-box plainly marked "Germany."

In 1936, Sears, Roebuck and Company advertised a "Colonial Figure Lamp" which was described as made of white china with colored decorations. A fancy flowered shade was included and an off-and-on snap button, also. The price, complete, was $1.00! Depression times were here.

In 1957, the date of another Daniel Low catalog we possess, there are no figural lamps advertised and boudoirs seem to be out of fashion. Hobnail milk glass lamps called "Early American" were the thing in the 1950's, and figural lamps had nearly disappeared.

Perhaps the exceptions are those lamps made in Occupied Japan, for when economic blockades were removed following World War II, Japan's output to this country included items similar to those they were exporting back in the 1930's. According to Marian Klamkin in her book, *Made in Occupied Japan*, there was only a short period of about five years beginning in 1948 when goods for export were made and marked "Occupied Japan."

Like many china ornaments, the lamps made during the period of occupation seem closer in style to those of an earlier period before the war. As they're usually attached to wooden or metal bases, the marks may be hidden and the finer pieces are not easy to identify and can be mistaken for European ware. Klamkin points out that the larger, better quality figures made in Occupied Japan were those models generally used for lamp bases as well as for mantel and shelf decorations, and sometimes the only way a collector has of identifying a lamp without taking it off the base is to find a matching shelf piece with "Made in Occupied Japan" clearly marked on the bottom.

Most of these figural boudoir lamps were sold in pairs, frequently modeled in matching mirror images so that they complemented each other when placed on opposite ends of the dressing table or bureau.

Check today's mail order gift catalogs and one finds only a figural lamp for a child's room or something in garish taste for the home bar. The happy ceramic imbiber draped around a lamp post takes precedence over the elegant 18th Century porcelain couple. What is there made today for the genteel pretensions of the first years of this century? Indeed, who remembers the illusion of that quiet, private room which few American housewives ever really had? Where is the boudoir today? In how many ranch houses, split-levels, apartments or condominiums can we find traces of that unique dream of grace and refinement? What has happened to the American version of a French boudoir, softly lit with a brace of fancy porcelain figural boudoir lamps?

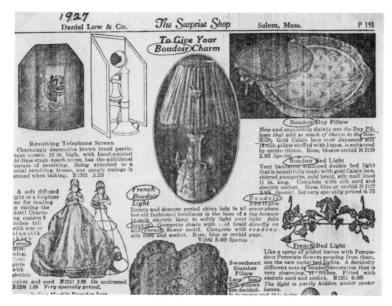

On half a page of this 1927 mail order catalog, the word "French" is used four times, and the word "Boudoir" appears nine times!

7077

Collection of Norma Werner

This googlie-eyed trio clinging together in hilarious desperation is a departure in design from the genteel, old-fashioned ladies we usually find holding up the light fixtures. Hardly a typical French boudoir lamp!

$50.00-100.00

34

Collection of Joyce Mineart   *Photo by Norma Werner*

One of the fine porcelain lamps from the Karl Schneider factory.

                     $50.00-100.00

Germany
5500

Collection of Mary Griffith
Photo by Norma Werner

A pretty duo of Mardi Gras figures dressed as Columbine and Pierrot. The hand-painted flowers and gold trim are indicative of work done by Ernst Bohne Sohne, Rudolstadt, but without more documentation we can only guess.

$100.00-150.00

Collection of Mrs. Ralph Renwick
Photo by Norma Werner

Not all designers of boudoir lamps modeled Old-Fashioned Ladies with ruffled skirts. This Mardi Gras figure wears a wildly bizarre costume topped by a Jester's cap.

Up to $50.00

77756

Dresden

Collection of Joyce Mineart   Photo by Norma Werner

With bird in hand (a dove, perhaps?), this ravishing creature could hold her place amid a bevy of boudoir lamp ladies.

A number of factories throughout Germany used the word "Dresden" in their trademarks and we can't be sure which manufacturer used the one shown here.

$50.00-100.00

37

2993
∨

Collection of Mrs. Ralph Renwick   Photo by Norma Werner

*A charming pair; one lady strums her lute while the other gazes dreamily into the distance.
Although the formal bouquet held by the dreamy young lady is really too large to be called a nosegay, the total effect is of delicacy and refinement and strikes the proper note for
even the most fastidious French boudoir.*

Marked as shown, with "Bavaria" stamped in green.

$50.00-100.00

38

Collection of Mary Griffith
Photo by Norma Werner

This angular, stylistic Pierrot handles his musical instrument in a most unorthodox manner, his left hand carelessly draped over the strings.

Considerable gold trim heightens the festive effect of the yellow, green, lavender and pink decoration.

Incised "16766."

Up to $50.00

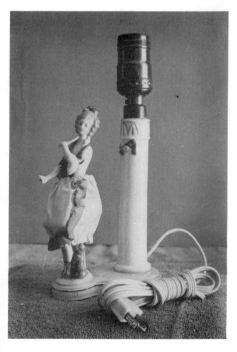

Collection of Nancy Klix

A novel combination, the lady is a porcelain half-figure fastened to a pincushion mid-riff. Her porcelain legs are modeled onto the lamp base.

Impressed on the base are the words "MADE IN GERMANY."

The lamp column is identical in design to that of the old-fashioned lady and her dog, so we might assume that the pieces came from the same factory.

$50.00-100.00

Collection of Charlotte Bill

Photo by Gene Tuck

A gentle lady in a chair, her pet dog scrambling up beside her, this charming lamp base is incised "Germany" as our only clue to its origin.

$50.00-100.00

14720
GERMANY

Collection of Joyce Mineart   Photo by Norma Werner

A fine example of a Flower Girl design popular during the early 1920's, this young lady wears a dress of petals and leaves. There is even a tiny stem topping her close-fitting hat of blossoms and petals!

$50.00-100.00

Collection of Mrs. Ralph Renwick   *Photo by Norma Werner*

This dainty young lady wears a purple lustre frock.
Incised "15964/GERMANY" beneath the Karl Schneider mark.

$50.00-100.00

Collection of Norma Werner

Some boudoir lamps were just wire frames designed to be hung over the headboard of a bed, with a china half-doll fastened on top.

The lamp shade was generally covered by pink crepe de Chine which gave a soft, rosy light, and, if we may judge by the slightly scorched examples we've seen, created a fire hazard if they came into contact with the electric light bulb.

Up to $50.00

Collection of Norma Werner

Sold as Fulper vaporizers, these 7½" porcelain twins may be either incense burners or parts of the Fulper perfume lamps.

They are hollow and fully open at the bases, with small openings in the backs beneath the shoulder ruffles.

$50.00-100.00 pair

43

Collection of Mary Griffith   *Photo by Norma Werner*

    An elegant court lady with a parrot, this 7" porcelain lamp is marked as shown, telling us that it comes from the Voigt factory, Sitzendorf.

$50.00-100.00

Photo by Norma Werner from her collection

This handsome gentlemen is obviously waiting to hand his lady love the dainty nosegay he is holding. Very likely he's one of a pair and if the collector is lucky, some day she will be able to reunite him with his mate.

An astounding number of firms especially in Great Britain, used an anchor mark on their small china items, and we cannot positively identify this one in gold.

The fixture is mounted on a brass foundation.

$50.00-100.00

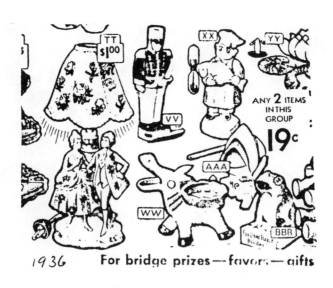

1936   **For bridge prizes — favors — gifts**

In 1936, Sears, Roebuck Company advertised a china Colonial Figure Lamp complete with fancy flowered shade for only a dollar. Courtesy of Marceil Drake.

Collections of Mary Griffith and Norma Werner   *Photo by Norma Werner*

Matching porcelain powder-box and lamp. The powder-box is stamped in red, "NANCY PERT/Dresser Dolls/ERPHILIA/Germany," and the lamp is incised "6175" and stamped in red "GERMANY." This same model has also been found in papier-mache as a candy box, marked "TERRE DE RETZ/MADE IN FRANCE."

$50.00-100.00 each

46

Collection of Charlotte Bill   *Photo by Gene Tuck*

This little two-tailed mermaid is our favorite figural lamp.
Marked with a crown and slashed initial "S", this 7" porcelain lamp base is a Sitzendorf product.

$100.00-150.00

47

16973
GERMANY

Collection of Mary Griffith
Photo by Norma Werner

In the early 1920's many gowns for evening wear had what was termed an "uneven hemline."

Here the modeler combined the mode with an 18th century look creating a dashing effect.

Up to $50.00

Photo by Norma Werner from her collection

A typical Lovely Lady china lamp made in Germany.

The colors of her gown are predominately shades of blue, but the yellow ruffles and trim, and the matching pink bow and fan, would blend with varied color schemes in numerous boudoirs of the times.

Up to $50.00

788
Germany

Photo by Norma Werner from her collection

Countless porcelain manufacturers used variations of a crown to mark their wares. This incised mark was probably used by the Sitzendorf factory of Alfred Voigt.

$50.00-100.00

49

Chapter Four
Pin Trays and Brushes

A figural pin tray is a *bona fide* dresser doll, that is if the little dish is actually modeled in the shape of a person. Most of those we've seen represent clowns, Pierrots or Columbines in a reclining position so that the figure's indented lap becomes the depression for holding pins, jewelry or face powder.

Some of the more imaginative dishes were made to hold powder-puffs which had handles shaped like legs, and the whole thing, when assembled, created a pretty porcelain lady with a swansdown skirt, kicking up her heels in light-hearted abandonment.

Probably the reason these figural dishes were not made in great quantity is that the subject was difficult to adapt to the form; the figures usually appear somewhat strained with the heads raised at an awkward angle. A graceful design was hard to achieve. Today young people are likely to assume that these figural dishes are ash trays, but early catalogs tell us otherwise. They were used on bureaus and dressing tables to hold small jewelry or powder, and they can still be useful as well as decorative.

Unlike china dishes, figural brushes cannot be complete in themselves but require the addition of bristles, whether the porcelain handle is designed as a full-length figure, a half-doll or only a head.

A surprising number of brushes, each with its own special use, was employed in the average household a few decades ago. It was not enough to have a whisk broom or clothes brush at hand; there must also be hat brushes and even glove brushes! Often the same model half-figure topping pincushions or cologne bottles would appear on brushes, and such sets are sought by today's collectors. When small dressing table brushes are found in good condition, they add an authentic touch to a collection of dresser dolls.

Collection of Norma Werner

Three clothes brushes with handles representing the fairy tale characters, Gretel, Hansel and Pinocchio.

These figures have been seen in china and composition, the latter material stained to give the appearance of polished wood. Approximately 8" overall.

Designed to encourage neatness at an early age.

Up to $50.00 each

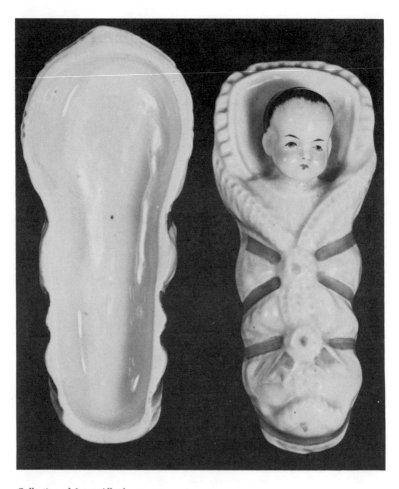

Collection of Joyce Allred

China pin dish with baby in swaddling blanket on lid, shown open.
This early dresser doll probably should be classified with the fairings, popular figural souvenirs of the 1880's.

$150.00-200.00

Collection of Florence Eikelberner   *Photo by Norma Werner*

   The complete dresser doll!
   This elegant porcelain half-doll holds two dishes for rings or small jewelry; she is fasten-
ed to a pincushion to store pins, needles and hat pins; her porcelain base includes a shallow
dish for powder or trinkets; and her head (with cork-stopper) comes off to reveal that her
upper body is also a perfume bottle.

53

$50.00-100.00

3900
Germany

Collection of Joyce Mineart   *Photo by Norma Werner*

The red jacket, turban and shoes, and the yellow blouse and full Turkish trousers are set off by touches of blue on the cuffs, turban ornament and trim around the edge of the pin tray. A charming dressing table accessory.

Up to $50.00

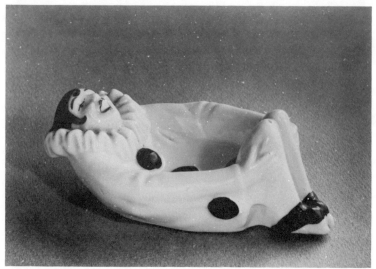

Collection of Bernadine Rink   *Photo by Lawrence James*

Nearly 5" long, this Pierrot powder dish is incised "6111" and is also marked "44" in brown paint.

A typical Pierrot with black skull cap, but unusual as the hair is painted brown.

$50.00-100.00

Collection of Chris Iwanski

6" long, incised "D.R.G.M.", this is an example of one of the many Flapper powder dish models. Missing are the porcelain legs attached to a powder-puff which would create the appearance of the reclining figure kicking her legs in the air.

In the November 1978 issue of "Half-Doll Happenings", Harriet Warkel shows us a sister model with arms behind her head.

Up to $50.00; with legs, $50.00-100.00

Collection of Verna Ortwine   Photo by Norma Werner

This lively pin tray is marked "NORITAKE/HAND PAINTED" with the initial "M" partially wreathed by a garland of leaves. Very attractive and desirable.

Up to $50.00

This brush top made of china closely resembles "Mr. Peanut", the trademark of the Planters Peanut Company, and may have been an advertising item.

Up to $50.00

Perhaps this brush with its china handle representing a dog's head was meant for a gentleman's dressing room.

Up to $50.00

Collection of Florence Eikelberner
Photo by Norma Werner

*7½" overall, this brush handle is a full length
figure dressed in a very fetching yellow two-
piece costume, complete with what the collector terms "harem pants."*
Incised "Germany."

Up to $50.00

Collection of Marceil Drake

*Small hat brush with china half-figure
stamped "Germany," fastened as a handle.
The hat and fur boa were very chic in 1927.*
Up to $50.00

Collection of Norma Werner

A handsome Pierrot powder dish, 5½" long, incised "23159/56." A swansdown puff with sterling silver handle came with the purchase.

A nearly identical figure is in the collection of Patricia Conn, but is painted with a white skull cap and shoes, and bears the Sitzendorf crown and slashed "S" of the Voigt manufacturing company.

$50.00-100.00

Chapter Five
Sewing Aids and Half-Dolls

In the United States, china half-figures have been called pincushion dolls simply because here so many of these little torsos were fastened on pincushions. Of course we know that they topped many other useful articles and were, in fact, frequently sold unassembled, leaving the buyer free to attach them to whatever she fancied. In Europe they often topped elaborate tea-cosies, and since one model might be made in several sizes, it is not uncommon to find a 6" half-doll on a tea-cosie and her 4" counterpart on a pincushion, while a 2½" example of the same design might turn up as the handle on a powder-puff.

Yet not all figural pincushions were assembled with half-doll tops. Sometimes we find a full-length, upright figure mounted on a padded, box-shaped pincushion, or a china figurine with a pincushion incorporated into the design, perhaps on top of the head to form a hat!

Such sewing aids found favor with china manufacturers and their customers in the early years of this century. Little figural tape measures, thimble containers and other small items useful in the bedroom were also popular, so it's not surprising that many figural sewing articles were made similar in design and style to the larger dresser dolls.

Porcelain sewing boxes with interior divisions for scissors, thimbles, spools of thread and other implements are often mistaken for powder-boxes until opened. Generally these had china figures on their lids and were not in human shape. They are somewhat scarce but, like the little china thimble boxes, they can be recognized for what they are when their lids are lifted and the neatly shaped partitions are in view.

Although not as plentiful as powder and trinket-boxes, all of these china figural sewing aids are delightful adjuncts to a dresser doll collection.

59

For the Boudoir

A dozen intimate and personal gifts for your feminine friends

SACHET
DESIGNS BY
ELIZABETH
MACKENZIE
ROTH

She is both frivolous and useful

TINY flowers painted on organdie over pink crêpe de Chine seem singularly fitting for the sweetness of sachet bags. The larger bag above holds a number of tiny sachet cakes, each encased in a little painted slip of its own and all ready to be distributed in dresser drawers.

The three lace-edged sachets in their varied shapes at the right are fascinatingly painted in soft colors; the six designs illustrated will be sent for fifteen cents. Please order H-531.

THE bouffant taffeta skirts of the little dame above conceal a round trinket box for the dresser. The silk is held to the box and the cover by means of gold braid and may be sewed to any pretty doll head of china such as can be bought in art needlework departments of large stores.

THREE tones of rose ribbon crushed close hold the scent in the heart of the delicate sachet at the left; the rest is just a frill of lace and two interesting leaves which are made of green and silver-barred ribbon.

Courtesy of Marceil Drake

A page from the December 1925 issue of the Woman's Home Companion *gives instructions for using a china half-doll to cover a trinket box for the dressing table.*

The model shown was coded MW 617-401 in The Collector's Encyclopedia of Half-Dolls.

Collection of Irma Bartell
Photo by Rita Harnish

This 2" half-doll and her china legs were made in Japan, and she is a copy of a favorite German model. The illustration shows how the parts were attached to a pincushion to give the illusion of a seated figure.

This is a factory produced assembly. Sometimes a lacy skirt was sewn around the half-doll's waist, partially concealing the legs.
Up to $50.00

Collection of Verna Ortwine
Photo by Norma Werner

One method of making a fancy figural pincushion was to fasten a half-doll onto a firmly stuffed middle piece, and then mount the whole onto a porcelain base with legs making the pedestal. Pins and needles could be hidden under the skirt, but more often were stuck through the flounces. Here the original satin ribbon and net show signs of wear, although the bisque lady maintains her composure.

The base is marked "D.R.G.M./MADE IN GERMANY."

$50.00-100.00

Collection of Wilma Saylor
Photo by Dern Studio

*A very fine porcelain half-figure, nearly 6",
more likely to be found on an elegant tea-cosie
than a lowly pincushion.*

*The applied flowers, excellent modeling, gold
trim and hand-painted bodice decorations all
denote expert craftsmanship.*

*Incised "9199", she is probably the product
of Ernst Bohne Sohn.*

$300.00-350.00

Collection of Kay and Harry Tattersall

*Half-dolls with modeled bodices were also
sewn onto pincushions, although in Europe they
more often were used on tea-cosies.*

*Apparently one of a series wearing European
folk costume, this 4" half figure represents a
young woman from Krautgersheim.*

*Incised "Germany/14344," with the printed
legend "Fabrique en Allemagne" inside the
base.*

$50.00-100.00

Collection of Frieda Marion

A 5" porcelain half-figure manufactured by the Karl Schneider company in Germany, coded MW 326-501, in The Collectors Encyclopedia of Half-Dolls.

Nude half-dolls were sold to be fastened on-to some useful object, in this country usually a pincushion. Fancy skirts were added, and a bodice made of ribbons or lace was sewn on-to the torso.

$100.00-150.00

Collection of Bernadine Rink
Photo by Lawrence James

Although the little china head is only 2¼", the entire assembly is over 12". All original, made in Germany.

The lower velvet pincushion was probably meant to hold long hat pins. A desirable col-lectible from the 1920's.

$50.00-100.00

63

Collection of Margaret Martin

Here the lady and the pincushion base are modeled as one, with a velvet covered cushion stuffed into the opening of what might otherwise have been an inkwell.

4½" high; marked "Made in Germany" in a round symbol on the base.

Up to $50.00

Collection of Norma Werner

Little girl in a tub; the velvet pincushion proves her usefulness even though she would be a welcome guest on any dressing table.

Up to $50.00

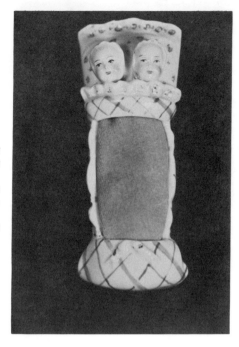

Collection of Joyce Allred

A fine example of early dresser dolls, these twins modeled in their porcelain cradle have a blue velvet pincushion for their blanket.

Probably of English origin, the 4" long piece is both attractive and desirable to today's collectors of antiques.

$150.00-200.00

Collection of Ruth Joyce

This 4½" bisque lady, dressed only in her dainty combinations, tops a square pincushion covered with pink silk.

She leans against a bisque column which is incised "0 7 E" and is also marked "Germany." The broken fan in her hand matches the color of her pale blue stockings.

$100.00-150.00

65

Collection of Norma Werner

A copy of the 1925 G. Sommers & Co. wholesale catalog shows small bisque dolls advertised as "suitable for pincushion, fancy articles, toys, etc."(American Collector Dolls, Westbrook/Ehrhardt.)

This is our proof that little play dolls were also used as dresser dolls under some circumstances.

4½" all bisque doll with pincushion covering. Up to $50.00

Collection of Bern Brekas
Photo by Tony Brekas

A 2¼" china cat with green glass eyes guards the dressing table amid a forest of pins. Up to $50.00

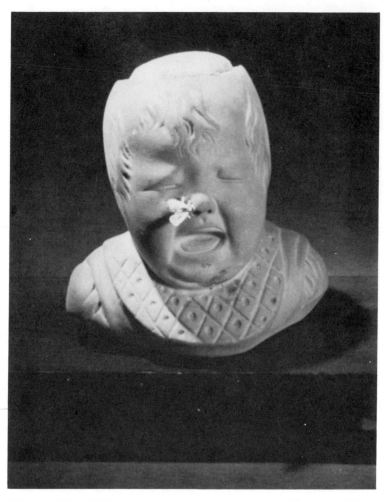

Collection of Bess Goldfinger   *Photo by Josh Segal*

The pincushion is in the top of the head of this 3½" crying infant. Made of terra cotta, the baby has a tiny bee on his nose.

Stamped "1184/G.D./Paris/depose," the head was made by Monsieur Delcroix who manufactured such articles at Montreuil around the 1880's.

A cloth bonnet covers the pincushion when not in use.

Collectors view this little item with mixed reactions.

$150.00-200.00

Collection of Mary Griffith

This little Pierrette head with her wide open mouth was probably a sewing aid to hold a tape measure or ribbons.

2" high, incised "15376/GERMANY."

Up to $50.00

68

This 3½" china figure of a child in Pierrot costume has a tape-measure fitted into the base.
Up to $50.00

Hat topped by a red velvet pincushion, this 3" bisque sailor boy sits patiently by the busy seamstress, eager to help.
Incised "MADE IN JAPAN."
Up to $50.00

Collection of Florence Eikelberner   *Photo by Norma Werner*

This 2" china head manages to retain her cool and austere expression in spite of the ludicrous arms and legs of ribbon, and the bulky pincushion body. This assembly is a prime example of a once popular sewing aid, but the choice of such a dignified head seems inappropriate.
$50.00-100.00

Chapter Six
Bottles and Stoppers

As anyone selling antiques or collectibles knows, figural bottles have been around for a long time. Historical whiskey flasks, for instance, are both very desirable and expensive. Fancy syrup jugs and medicine or ink bottles are among the many liquid containers made in human shape. In his erudite book, *Dolls and Puppets*, Max von Boehm devotes a chapter to "Utensils in Doll Form" in which he has a good deal to say about the ancient art of producing pots and vessels in human form from such materials as bronze, glass, wood or clay. Of course not all such artifacts were intended to grace Milady's boudoir where we've been prying around in a previous chapter.

The figural bottles that sat on dainty dressing tables were made of decorated porcelain and were meant to hold perfume or cologne. In design they are as beautiful, charming or whimsical as the vanity-boxes, the pincushion dolls or the small figural lamps, all of which we call dresser dolls.

The basic design of a figural bottle was that of a young lady modeled in two separate sections. When the head or upper body was removed, there was revealed an attached cork stopper with glass dauber. The skirt and lower body formed the hollow container for liquid.

Numerous variations were developed from this simple design, including some bottle ladies with holes in the top of their heads. A removable hat or a metal crown might then constitute the bottle stopper.

If the boudoir owner was fortunate to have space for a writing desk (preferably Louis XIV in style), she would then have reason to show off a pretty figural inkwell. She might also keep at hand a perfume vial with a tiny china head for the stopper. Fancy stoppers have their own history as figural items. To be sure, grotesque carved wooden heads are often for sale in gift shops today, but porcelain stoppers of varied human design have their own appeal and were once quite the rage.

A torn, undated page from an old magazine, sent by my colleague, Norma Werner, advertises a set of boxed bottle stoppers in the shape of ladies' legs, the complete set selling for only $4.25. To be accurate, the printed caption designates these stoppers as girls' gams.

"For centuries," reads the ad, "it seems there has been a crying need for bottle stoppers in the shape of a girl's gams . . . At last . . . a set of three, gift-boxed. How happy you will be to have these chinaware bijous, 5" high, with hand-decorated gold slippers! (But will your hooch taste better?)." Hooch?

My fifth edition of *Webster's Collegiate Dictionary*, 1936, defines the word "hooch" as U.S. slang meaning "crude, ardent spirits, esp. surreptitiously made or obtained." Surely these girl-gam stoppers have no place in our ladies' boudoirs!

Yet we must admit that there were some ladies, even during Prohibition days, who now and then took a little nip if only for medicinal purposes. In the October 1969 issue of *Old Bottles*, Roberta Starry's article tells us just how they got away with it then without disturbing those refined boudoir decorations. Ms. Starry's feature pointed out how many a china figure similar to a vertical trinket-box easily concealed a small flask, and the illustrations accompanying her article are most graphic. As for those perfume vials mentioned above, some were made with double containers; the top came off to release a drop of perfume all right, but the silver ferrule below could be twisted to let out the entire tube of perfume, "leaving a sizable shot of liquor in the innocent looking vial."

According to the author of this fascinating story, many very imaginative containers for liquor bottles were devised during Prohibition, some of which had openings that you had to be sober to work. She suggests these items as the "ultimate in conversation pieces" for bottle collectors who have everything. It makes us wonder how many of the cologne bottles or tall trinket boxes we've examined were really produced to conceal a little hooch in case milady felt a bit faint as she whiled away the time in her boudoir. Perhaps we'd all better take another look at our collections of porcelain figural bottles to determine if they're really as innocent as they seem.

Collection of Harriet Warkel   *Photo by Brian L. Lowe*

Three piece set of powder box and perfume and cologne bottles.
Sales catalogs show us that these sets came with numerous pieces, but without the manufacturers' records we can't be sure how many other items might be matched. Ring boxes, brushes, pin trays, pincushions and lamps might also be part of a set, so the collector is constantly watching for new treasures to turn up.

$100.00-150.00 set

Collection of Eleanor Harriman
Photo by David Hayden

What a treasure we have in this young woman in her brightly colored peasant costume and dashing stance!

When taken apart she reveals a ceramic receptacle for ink inside her skirt, and at her feet there's a modeled slot for a pen.

She's marked "ERPHILA/INK GIRLS/Germany," with the numeral '6002."

Such positive documentation is the researcher's delight.

$50.00-100.00

Collection of Maxine Burkholder

A 4" china perfume bottle which clearly shows that the lady's torso is the stopper.

Up to $50.00

Collection of Eleanor Harriman   *Photo by David Hayden*

The lady and the bird. This china figural perfume bottle features a court lady sitting on a stool, holding a cockatoo in her right arm. The gold crown on the bird's head forms the stopper.

Scarcely 4" high, she is a very pleasing dresser doll.

Up to $50.00

4367 Germany.

Collection of Norma Werner

How casually she courtseys, with little regard for the fact that she may spill her perfumed brains from the unstoppered hole in her head!

Besides the mark shown, she bears a red stamped trademark of a crown within a wreath and the words "CORONET" and "REGISTERED/GERMANY."

Up to $50.00

75

Collection of Joyce Mineart

Here Pierrot is a little porcelain perfume bottle, less than 3" high. His white suit is accented by the blue trimming on the ruff, and the large black buttons, shoes and skull cap.
Made in Germany. (Stopper missing.)
Up to $50.00

Collection of Norma Werner

A bottle stopper, this china head of a laughing man wearing a red cap would hardly fit into a proper boudoir, but might be used by the man of the house in his liquor cabinet.
Up to $50.00

JAPAN

76

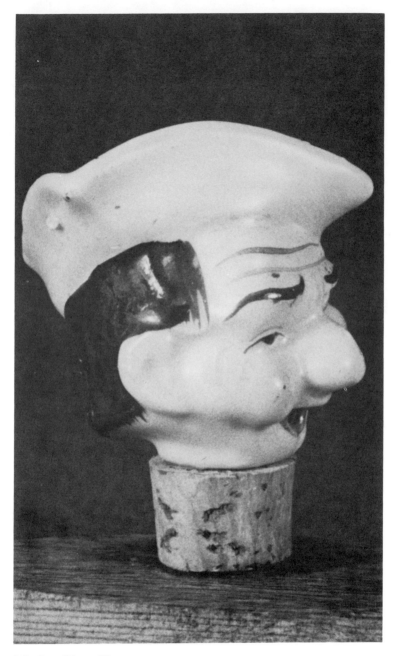

Collection of Norma Werner

Similar to carved wooden heads, this grotesque china head is fitted with a cork and pours through the opened mouth.

Up to $50.00

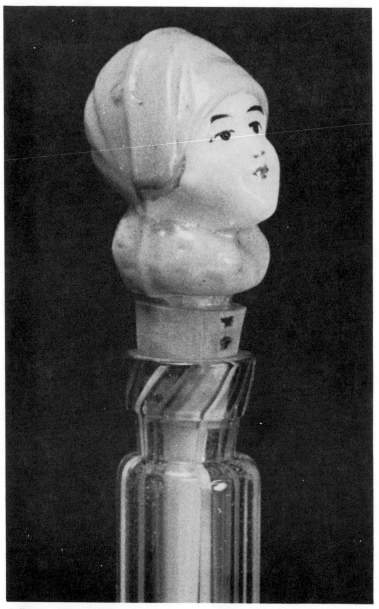

Collection of Norma Werner

   Blown glass perfume vial with china head stopper complete with cork and long glass dauber. The head is only 1" high.

   The Flapper head is tres chic *in her blue cloche and little fur neckpiece. A gem from the 1920's.*

   The vial is stamped "GERMANY."

Up to $50.00

Collection of Wilma Jo Saylor   *Photo by Dern Studio*

Although first listed in our files as a tea-caddy, this china figural container so closely resembles those shown in Roberta Starry's article we are including it in our chapter on bottles. Obviously this 9" piece could easily conceal a small liquor bottle while maintaining a stylish appearance on the dressing table.

$50.00-100.00

Collection of Dorothy Trumbull

Left: The little girl wrapped in a shawl is a perfume bottle with the spout protruding from the top of her head. A metal and cork stopper completes the piece.

Right: Shawl, folded hands and hanging purse are identical, but this young lady is a "nodder" with her head attached by a rubber band allowing it to swivel and bob.

Incised "GERMANY."

Up to $50.00 each

Collection of Wilma Jo Saylor   *Photo by Dern Studio*

A pair of 5" cologne bottles representing the character Pierrot from the classic Commedia dell Arte, marked "BAVARIA." Paper stickers denote the importer, Irving W. Rice of New York, and indicate that he registered the design, so that it's probable that his firm financed the production of these porcelain bottles.

A matching cigarette holder was shown in The Collector's Encyclopedia of Half-Dolls.

$100.00-150.00 pair

80

Collection of Norma Werner

A most unusual dresser doll; the upper part of the body lifts off like a powder-box, reveal-ing the cork stoppered opening in the skirt which forms the bottle.

Dressed in pink and cream, with white ruffled apron and black ribbons, she is a joy to behold!

Up to $50.00

Collection of Norma Werner

Two pieces of a dressing table set. Left: 4½" china perfume bottle, with hole in the top of the lady's bouquet for the missing stopper.

Right: 5" powder-box with figural perfume bottle modeled onto the lid. The metal device on the bouquet opening suggests that there was originally an atomizer attached here.

The mark is that used by the Sitzendorph factory of the Voigt brothers.

Up to $50.00 each

Collection of Maxine Burkholder

A cologne bottle in an appealing child design. The head is the stopper.
3" high.

Up to $50.00

Collection of Marie Burdick

A colorful 6" china perfume bottle which was very likely part of a dresser doll set. With little change in the design, this model would make a handsome boudoir lamp.

Such pieces are a fascinating challenge to the serious collector.

$50.00-100.00

Chapter Seven
Little China Heads

Charming and versatile, the little china heads of the dresser doll era constitute a special category for today's collector who looks for novelty in miniature. Many were used as powder-puff handles or bottle stoppers, or were fastened to little boxes as knobs to raise the lids. Others came on pencils in sets accompanying playing card tally-pads. All are under the general heading of dresser dolls although, unless they were made to conceal something useful such as a tape measure or thimble, they really aren't complete household articles but, like half-dolls, are only decorative additions.

Rarely over two inches high, little china heads can be overlooked at antique shows or yard sales but may be discovered by the persistent collector who goes poking about in old candy boxes or other accumulations of odds and ends. Sometimes an uninterested seller mistakes a little head for part of a broken doll and prices accordingly.

To be sure, clever collectors may fashion stuffed cloth bodies for these heads thus making them into tiny dolls to occupy their dolls' houses. Some heads have sew-holes in their bases, so it's easy to fasten them securely to the chosen object; others have a flange to facilitate the attachment.

Flat-heads (china heads in bas-relief) were also popular novelties, and these were sewn onto cosmetic cases or to large cloth envelopes in which lingerie or nightwear were stored. Flat-heads were also sold in kits which the busy needlewoman, with a nudge from the "Modern Priscilla," could make up into various wall-hangings useful as hosiery bags, guest towel racks, or other prettified necessities.

Like half-dolls, little china heads came in a variety of models to appeal to a broad market and many were sold to decorate hand-made gifts. Over fifty years ago, a little satin sachet pillow adorned with a tiny porcelain face in bas-relief made a welcome gift for a lady's boudoir. We like to think that these little heads can still be appreciated today.

Collection of Norma Werner

An unusual large head, 3½", which suggests that the designer intended an Oriental figure. The brows are painted both black and brown with visible brush strokes, the eyelids are modeled as well as painted, as are the teeth. The head is painted black with no clue as to whether it is a cap or the figure's hair.

$50.00-100.00

Collection of Norma Werner

Of course not everyone could wear a hat like this, but in 1923 Paul Poiret included a similar style to top off an improbable "walking costume." "The Decorative Twenties" by Martin Battersby, shows us other similar hats designed by Marthe Regnier for film actress Gloria Swanson in 1925.

2" of very high fashion.

$50.00-100.00

Collection of Bern Brekas

    The hats are pink with wide white bands, and it is no wonder that some collectors seek little china heads just to show off the head gear!

    The bobbed hair is light brown and the heavy-lidded eyes are blue. The long necks were made to rise fastidiously above swansdown powder-puffs.

Up to $50.00 each

Collection of Dolly Salisbury
Photo by Regal

    Anita Loos once told us that gentlemen prefer blondes, no doubt referring to someone like this frivolous young thing with her yellow hair, pink hat, and amourous glance.

    2" high, incised "Germany/5880."

Up to $50.00

87

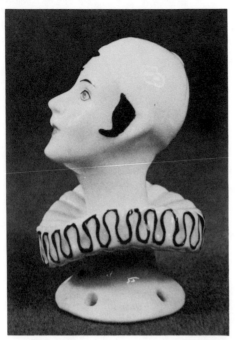

Collection of Florence Eikelberner

Although the little Pierrot heads generally have a black skull cap, a few models are found in white and most of these are called Pierrettes in reference to their longer necks and more feminine features.

This model is 2½" high and incised "95."
Up to $50.00

Collection of Isabella Gravitt

Two points make this china head desirable to collectors: it represents a child and also a clown or Mardi Gras design.

Under 2", marked "Germany/595," it was originally on a lamb's wool puff.
Up to $50.00

88

Collection of Patricia Conn

Like half-figures, china heads were modeled to depict various historical and literary
characters, and this is believed to be the Pied
Piper of Hamlin, subject of Robert Browning's
poem of the same name.
   2½" high; incised "24449/Germany."
                        $50.00-100.00

Collection of Norma Werner

Under 2", this exotic lady with her auburn
hair is a fine example of the charm and variety of little china heads.
                        $50.00-100.00

89

Collection of Marie Burdick

Lady with a turban, this small china head is an example of the variety to delight the collector.

$50.00-100.00

Collection of May Wenzel
Photo by Helen Barglebaugh

This 2½" china bas-relief has three sew-holes with which it's fastened to a large, long-handled pink puff. Perfect for the lady who has time to indulge in the luxury of powdering the small of her back!

$50.00-100.00

Collection of Norma Werner

A small china bas-relief called a "flat-head" by collectors, this one was purchased sewn onto a lace-trimmed pillow.

The wide brimmed hat was all the rage in the 1920's but too difficult for the decorators to cope with, so that they invariably painted one eye lower than the other rather than struggle with the effect of it shaded by the drooping brim.

Up to $50.00

7194

6840

Collection of Florence Eikelberner
Photo by Norma Werner

A 3" bas-relief, incised "6840/Germany," this little china head was sold in a kit with instructions to make a guest towel holder or a small hosiery bag.

In spite of her sophisticated appearance, the directions given were for an embroidered frock most suitable for the very young girl of the sweet old-fashioned type.

$50.00-100.00

Collection of Norma Werner

A small bisque mask with sew-hole on top and beneath chin, this face closely resembles play dolls of the early 1900's. Inset glass eyes and open mouth with teeth, she needs a wig to complete her charm.

Found on an old cushion. Unmarked.

Up to $50.00

Collection of Marjorie Stark
Photo by Ron Titus

This 1¾" china head came complete with an old price tag identifying him as the Prince of Wales, and the incised "P.o.W." across the front bears out the description. Also incised "24865."

Very smart in his blue naval officers' jacket and gold banded cap, he represents Edward VIII who abdicated in 1936 and became the Duke of Windsor.

Written on the tag is "Prince of Wales Puff," explaining his function in the dresser doll world. The tag is also stamped "MADE IN ENGLAND" and on the reverse is the date "Feb. 23, 1926."

In 1926, the year before Lindbergh flew the Atlantic, the Prince of Wales was the world's most desirable bachelor.

$200.00-250.00

Collection of Frieda Marion
Photo by Chris Fraser

Less than 2" of insouciance, the lady in her mauve colored cloche and gold dangling earrings was quite the thing in 1925.

Up to $50.00

Collection of Joyce Mineart

Stylized Pierrette head, 2" high, incised "746."
This irresistible creature with her long lashes and heart-shaped mouth, was no doubt made to be a powder-puff handle.

$50.00-100.00

93

Chapter Eight
Bathing Beauties and "Sew-Ons"

"Bathing Beauties" is a very loose term designating little figurines generally clothed only in the bathing caps and slippers worn before the 1920's. As with all our attempts to classify these china pieces, it's difficult to do so with precision. "Nudies" is a name some collectors favor, but nudie doesn't really apply to those bathing beauties who do wear painted bathing dresses. Then there are those provocative little nude figures complete with high heeled shoes! Bathing slippers were flat, of course, and surely the fancy high heels were not intended for beach wear.

Most bathing beauties are bisque, although we do find some that are glazed. Some have wigs. Other nudes are actually figurines that are complete as shelf pieces, and still others, although similar, have bases with sew-holes and were clearly meant to be fastened to something more useful.

We suspect that many of these nude figures were intended to be displayed only in the den or bedroom, and in most households they were never exhibited in the parlor or family sitting-room. Those with sew-holes often languished in the bedroom amid ruffles and lace on pillows or nightwear cases, and some, like the two-tailed mermaid shown on page 103, may have been designated for the goldfish bowl.

Full-length sew-ons, whether nude or dressed, were almost as plentiful as china heads and half-dolls, and like the latter were manufactured to be attached to whatever suited the buyer. The same companies that produced figural powder-boxes, lamps, bottles, pin trays, brush handles, and all of the china articles mentioned in this book also made bathing beauties and little full-length figures with sew-hole bases.

In the early 20th century the lady of the house could hardly complain of being alone, surrounded as she was by these spritely china images gazing at her with painted eyes from every shelf and bureau and dressing-table. Dresser dolls of one sort or another invaded not only the private boudoir but, as we shall see, had a place in the kitchen or on the tea table.

Collection of Joyce Mineart   Photo by Norma Werner

Nude in pink slippers.
What can we make of this 6½" bisque lady with her provocative glances from her intaglio blue eyes, her lips parted in an alluring smile, her fine mohair wig caught carelessly in a net snood? Surely her place was in the boudoir and not the family living room!
Incised "11954."

$150.00-200.00

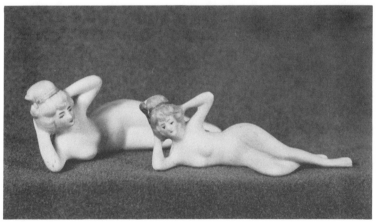

Collection of Mary Griffith

Adorned only in pink and maroon hair ribbons, two langorous bisque nudes recline in the boudoir.
Marks are indecipherable.

$50.00-100.00 each

95

Collection of Joyce Mineart   Photo by Norma Werner

Whoops! What goes on here?
This exuberant bisque lady was found clothed in tattered net decorated with a metallic
bow at her middle. She was modeled nude except for her pink ballet slippers.
She wears a fine mohair wig.
3½" high.

96                                    $150.00-200.00

Collection of Marciel Drake

Little boy clown in a yellow hat 3" high; incised "25064."

Up to $50.00

Germany

Collection of Norma Werner

1½" child figure in yellow clown costume with orange trim. The base with sew-holes tells us that this tiny china item was made to be fastened to some household article.

Marked as shown.

Up to $50.00

Collection of Norma Werner

A first glance this tiny figure in bathing suit and cap appears to be a figurine or shelf piece, but close examination shows a base which is very narrow in front but wide enough in back to have one hole for fastening onto another object.

Very colorful in her orange swim suit and green cap. No marks.

Under 2" in height, she might top a number of things.

Up to $50.00

Collection of Vicki Halliday

The distinguishing feature of this china "sew-on" is her gold necklace which she begs us to admire. With her blonde hair and blue dress she is irresistible.

2½" high, incised "14595/Germany."

Up to $50.00

Collection of Mary Griffith   Photo by Norma Werner

Left: top hatted little boy holding a bouquet of pink roses under each arm. Incised "15140/GERMANY."   Up to $50.00

Right: similar 'sew-on' china figure, holding an unknown object. Incised "14851/GERMANY."   Up to $50.00

Both are 3" high. A nearly identical figure wearing a cap with pom-pom was shown in China Half-Figures Called Pincushion Dolls. A study of a number of these models as well as several of smaller size, suggests to the authors that they belong to a group made by Karl Schneider and may have been reissued some years after they were first introduced.

Collection of Eleanor Harriman   Photo by Richard Merrill

Left: a plump Pierrot perfume bottle, 3" high, must use his head for a stopper.
                                                                            Up to $50.00

Right: a languishing Columbine, 8" long, is made to be sewn onto a pillow or nightgown case.
Collector Sarah Westlund owns a matching Pierrot, 8½" long, incised with the Karl Schneider trademark, which would go nicely on a pajama case. (Collector's Encyclopedia of Half-Dolls, page 535.)

99   *$250.00-300.00*

This little china devil, only 2¼" high, surely is a true Imp of Satan in his painted black outfit complete with bat wings and horns.

Incised "Germany/14541," the same model has been found painted bright orange-red.

Like half-dolls, full figures were made to be fastened onto useful household objects and were produced with base holes to facilitate attachment.

$150.00-200.00

This 2½" porcelain "sew-on" represents the popular French dancer Gaby Deslys, internationally known during the 1920's.

Many souvenirs were sold to Gaby's fans during her day, most of them showing her in this position with the same coy expression and sidelong glance.

A touching story about the dancer was written by doll dealer Joan Hunter in the English magazine Living Dolls, published by Carol Ann Stanton.

$100.00-$150.00

Collection of Bern Brekas
  2¼" Mardi Gras girl, incised "76."

Up to $50.00

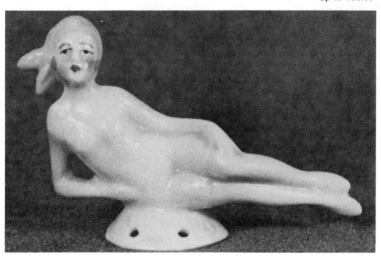

Collection of Mary Griffith

A true bathing beauty in her white suit and blue bandana, this 2½" long china "sew-on" would be a lively decoration on top of a number of boudoir articles.
  Incised "Germany 5750."

Up to $50.00

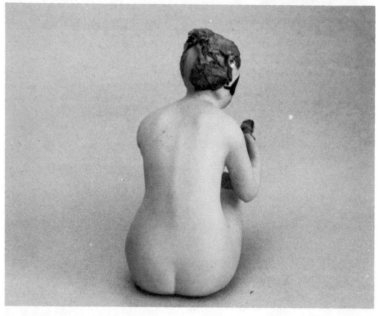

Collection of Patricia Hartwell

    An elegant bisque nude, this charming lady wearing high heeled shoes, painted stockings and a modeled Domino mask, is 4½" long and 3¼" high.

    Holding a single rose, her head is wrapped in the original shipping paper, in lieu of a wig for eventual display. A beauty spot on her right cheek completes her adornment.

$300.00-350.00

Collection of Frieda Marion

Tiny bisque bathing beauties wearing yellow bathing slippers.
Left: 3½" long. Incised "Germany/4375."
Right: the added attraction is an orange bathing cap. Marked "Germany/2030."

Up to $50.00 each

Collection of Mary Griffith

A pensive mermaid with a double tail! Was she destined for the goldfish bowl?
Incised "8/JAPAN."

Up to $50.00

103

Collection of Florence Eikelberner

A glazed nude figure, 4½" long, modeled with a sew-hole base so that she can be sewn onto a pillow or large pincushion.

We doubt if these ladies were meant to be costumed, but modesty sometimes compelled the owners to drape them in ribbons and laces.

Up to $50.00

Collection of Florence Eikelberner

About 4" long, this little blonde sun bather is in the class some collectors term "nudies." Marked "Germany."

104

Up to $50.00

Chapter Nine
Tea Table Items

In *Doll News*, the official publication of the United Federation of Doll Clubs, Inc., the August 1956 issue printed an advertisement for Ice Cream Ladies, the "party favor supreme."

These little half-dolls, offered by Esther F. Barnard, were made expressly to top a mound of ice cream and were described by her as "Cast in my own formula Blonde Porcelain. Bisque Finish hand painted. Your favorite Ice Cream Dealer has the mould for the skirt. He will add the ruffles and the color to match your dolls costuming. Size of doll 1¾ inches - $1.50 each - $15.00 dozen. Meet me in my booth at the Convention."

A pencilled margin notation by collector Bern Brekas who contributed this clipping states "Never did buy one," so we have no record of the quality of these porcelain Ice Cream Ladies and, in fact, we're not even sure if Bern actually ever met Esther in her booth at the Convention.

But surely somebody did, and since the Ice Cream Ladies were advertised as party favors, the lucky guests must have taken them home when the festivities were over. Some of these delectable favors must still exist SOMEwhere.

The faded illustration shows that the porcelain Ice Cream Ladies were each placed on individual servings of the dessert, rather like the luncheon salad half-dolls of which Flora Gill Jacobs wrote, *(China Half-Figures Called Pincushion Dolls*, Marion, page 59.) Flora's mother used half-dolls made in Germany, but obviously Esther was selling her own products which may have been reproductions but, from the hair styles, could have been her own original 1950's creations.

One slightly pessimistic note, Dear Reader: before sending out the invitations to your party, remember that even with a full supply of porcelain party favors supreme, you're going to have to snare your favorite ice cream dealer and make sure he has the proper mold for the skirts and is willing to add all those ice cream ruffles!

Most china figurals gracing the tea table remain with the hostess. Her teapot, for instance, might steam during an entire afternoon if covered with a thick tea-cosie skirt worn by a half-doll, but after the party both pot and cosie would be returned to the cupboard.

Directions for a knitted tea-cosie found in Dilys Winn's entertaining book, *Murderess Ink*, were pointed out to us by collector David Streeter. These are reprinted from yarn and wool dealers Patons & Baldwins Limited under the heading "Warming the Pot," because the author believes that lady detectives of the Miss Marple type find a knitting project indispensible. The accompanying illustration shows us a very bulky tea-cosie which effectively smothers the pot but does exhibit to good advantage a Colonial Lady china half-figure sewn on top.

In case working on this wooly tea-cosie isn't enough to occupy a female detective cogitating on crime, Winn mentions that six egg-cosie designs can also be obtained from the prestigious Patons & Baldwins Limited, but neglects to tell us where to purchase the half-dolls to top them off. Although egg-cosies have a limited appeal in the United States, there's no doubt they were once commonly used in Great Britain; and our English collector friends, Phyllis and Roy Pavitt, have a set of six, all with identical little girl half-dolls.

As if it wasn't enough to cover the teapot with a lady tea-cosie, manufacturers busied themselves producing china teapots in the shape of persons, usually pretty ladies in very wide skirts. In such cases the lid was modeled in the shape of head and torso, and the pot itself was the skirt.

We own one of these utensils with the skirt a series of china ruffles, the top one coyly draped to allow the spout of the pot to protrude for pouring. The handle on the opposite side is neatly molded onto the ruffles and as they're of floor length (or table length, if you prefer) we'll never know what happened to the lady's legs.

Figural teapots are not really rare, and even complete tea sets with matching figural sugar bowls or pitchers have often been produced with varying success. *English Pottery and Porcelain* by Geoffrey Wills tells us of a novel Worcester teapot, circa 1880, with a man's head modeled on one side and a woman's on the other!

Cookie jars, salt and pepper shakers, small jugs and pitchers, and little bells for the tea table have all been made of chinaware in the shape of human beings or animals. Here we've illustrated some of these dining room and kitchen items; it is up to the collector to choose what is most interesting and appropriate to develop an individual collection.

It is probably safe to say that a group of well designed china figurals popular during the early years of this century, if modeled in good proportion and decorated with care and good taste, will appreciate in value over the next few years in a moderate to rapid rate.

Collection of Joyce Mineart

Tiny china figural place card holders with slotted heads, this young lady and gentleman are part of a set all decorated in matching blue and yellow.

Marked "Germany," and "63" and "74" respectively.

Up to $50.00 each

Collection of Joyce Mineart

From a set of place card holders, a 2" high Pierrot and matching Pierrette, very colorful in their blue trimmed suits, yellow mandolins, and rosy cheeks and mouths.

Marked "Germany," and "67" and "66" respectively.

The slots for the place cards are across the tops of their heads.

Up to $50.00 each

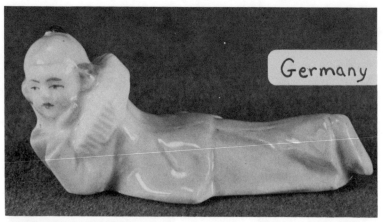

Germany

Collection of Joyce Mineart

A place card holder for lunch, this 3" long child clown makes an attractive bridge favor. The suit and shoes are pink, the neck ruff is white, and there is a black pom pom for accent on top of the pink cap.

A slot along the side holds a place card upright.

Up to $50.00

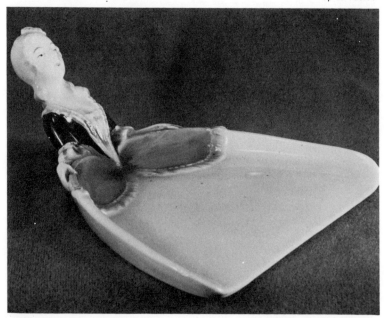

Collection of Norma Werner

Porcelain crumb tray representing a curtseying lady, marked twice by W. Goebel (once incised and once stamped.)

Another collector has written to tell us that she has seen the matching brush for this set.

$50.00-100.00

Collection of Norma Werner

3½" salt shaker stamped "JAPAN."
The orange dress and hat is painted with an iridescent glaze very popular on china during the 1920's and 30's.

Up to $50.00

Collection of Frieda Marion

    A teapot lady in a skirt of pale blue porcelain ruffles.
    Other figural teapots were produced by the Shawnee Potteries (1937-1961), according to information in the magazine Spinning Wheel, *1979.*

Up to $50.00

Collection of Marilyn Cunningham.

    A pair of fine salt and pepper shakers with applied flowers and gold decoration. The mark may be that of the porcelain factory of Adolf Persch, Hegewald.
    4½" high.

$50.00-100.00 set

110

Collection of Norma Werner

This dainty dancing belle is actually a 4" tea bell with a bisque clapper, reminding us of a more leisurely day when afternoon tea was served on the best quality table linen in French and Eyelet design.

When the last guest leaves, the lady of the house has only to ring the little tea bell for her maid (wearing a tea apron of the best quality French lawn), and retire to her boudoir, where she can relax beneath the rosy glow of her French boudoir lamps.

Or was it all just a dream?

Up to $50.00

Collection of Norma Werner

This pitcher, similar to the familiar Toby jugs in design, is marked with a gold anchor. Less than 4" high.

Up to $50.00

Collection of Norma Werner

This little girl with her orange hat is actually a 2-piece set consisting of a salt dip base and pepper shaker top. 2½" high.
Stamped "MADE IN JAPAN."

Up to $50.00

113

Collection of Norma Werner

Set of china figural salt and pepper shakers, and a jelly (or jam) jar, made in Germany.
Up to $50.00 for set

In the days when the term "Spring chicken" was used to describe a pretty young lady, someone tried to translate the epithet into what we might call a crude porcelain pun. The result was this Flapper-chicken 3½" salt shaker with holes in the back of her head.

Did feminists object? Certainly this was not a best-seller and is quite rare today.

Stamped "Germany."

Up to $50.00

A tiny bird made to perch on a teapot spout, attached to a padded "drip-catcher," this little blue bird has a wing spread of only 1½"

Drip-catcher figurals can be distinguished from powder-puff handles because the former have curved bases to fit onto the teapot spout

Up to $50.00

Collection of Patricia Conn

A handsome fighting cock, incised "Germany/7147," was destined to hold a drip-catcher to a teapot spout by means of a cord or elastic run through the holes in his base.
Up to $50.00

Collection of Patricia Conn

A most remarkable china cat teapot with a butterfly drip-catcher on her paw (spout).

Small birds and butterflies with their curved bases were used to attach a cushion to the teapot spout to absorb any drops, and these tiny figurals were often very detailed and colorful.

Dripcatcher, up to $50.00; teapot still in production

116

Chapter Ten
"Nippes"

The Germans have a word for them. Since most of the china figurals in this book were produced in Austria, Bavaria or Germany, it's not surprising that the German language has an appropriate word to cover the field. "Nippes" (knick-knacks or bric-a-brac) does very well.

In 1980, Gunter and Jutta Griebel sent me a copy of their colorful little book *Nippes: Madchen und Puppchen (Knick-knacks: Young Ladies and Dolls,* published in Munich and written, of course, in German. With the help of my sister Marise Fraser, who translated much of the text, I've learned from and enjoyed this book. Color illustrations show many models of lovely porcelain half-dolls, coy bathing beauties, novel hat pin holders and innumerable figures, all produced in Germany from 1870 to 1930.

One provocative chapter is called "Kunst oder Kitsch?," a phrase we can only translate as "Art or Kitsch?," for although we've given a fair rendering of the word **nippes**, there's really nothing quite as expressive as **kitsch** to use for those little china figurals which border on questionable taste. Fortunately the word kitsch has already been introduced to the English language so most readers have a good idea of its meaning.

No style is ever as tasteless as that which has just become outmoded, so any fashion recently passe is certainly kitsch from the contemporary viewpoint.

Art Deco, closely followed by Modernistic with its bold design and strong contrasts, swept away the dainty modes of the preceding years. Fancy china half-figures elegantly costumed in silks and laces lost favor and were replaced by half-dolls depicting Flappers or strange angular creatures inspired by the Diaghilev dancers. Then the craze for attaching models of the human form to anything and everything ceased to be "the thing."

In 1930 no one talked about being "in," but almost everyone was concerned about doing or having what was absolutely "the thing."

Popular novelist Katherine Brush gave us a marvelous picture of what was no longer the thing in the days when geometrical chic had supplanted aesthetic refinement.

In *Red-Headed Woman,* published in 1931, Brush described how Lillian, her central character, furnished her new home without the aid of a decorator because, as Lillian told her husband, she might not know all about art but she knew what she liked. Lillian obviously liked kitsch.

"The rooms were crowded to the doors with what Lillian liked," Brush wrote. "Brocaded satin chairs. Brocaded satin divans. Wrought-iron Spanish benches . . . Standing lamps with rosy fringed-silk shades." Lillian liked bric-a-brac and statuettes and framed reproductions of Maxfield Parrish pictures. Today Maxfield Parrish's work is again in favor, but in 1930 cubism had taken over and Parrish was out. Not so in the home of Brush's Red-Headed Woman whose bedroom had everything "down to the powder-puff container and the telephone doll . . . "

Ah, the telephone doll! A pretty bauble, the telephone doll was a porcelain half-figure assembled on a frame large enough so that her flowing skirt could conceal an upright telephone. A splendid decorating touch in Lillian's girlhood but, as the author makes clear, outmoded and unchic in the new modernism of the 1930's.

But although Lillian reveled in the kitsch of her day, it's doubtful if she would have displayed any of the little figures the Greibels label as "Scherz-figuren" in their book of nippes. These slightly risque models of comic themes, while not offending Lillian, would have had no place in a decorative scheme designed to impress everyone (ANYone!) with her new wealth and social position. Yet whether they're art or kitsch, the scherzfiguren of the 1920's are very collectible today.

While the German word "nippes" does cover the field well, we think that the finest figural boxes and lamps deserve better than to be dismissed as knick-knacks. Curios, objets d'art or bibelots are other terms sometimes used, but we think that most of the pieces in this book are generally referred to by today's collectors as dresser dolls, and as these figurals have a strong appeal to doll collectors, we've readily adopted the name.

Within this category the reader is aware of numerous specialties, from early fairings (figural souvenir boxes sold at fairs in the mid-1800's) to much later pieces from Occupied Japan following World War II. Of course fairings and 19th Century figurines have already received considerable attention from collectors and dealers, and are more often found in antique shops and shows than at flea markets or lawn sales. However, the later dresser dolls stressed here are still available and there is always the enticing possibility of treasures to be discovered or bargains struck for seekers who are diligent, knowledgeable and, we confess, lucky! Surprisingly, the more informed we become, the luckier we're apt to be.

Porcelain powder-boxes, figural boudoir lamps, half-dolls, bathing beauties, little china heads and various figural tea table utensils are all out there somewhere just waiting to be picked up and appreciated. All are part of a rising market and the best of them will be among the antiques of tomorrow.

How fortunate is the person today who, for a modest expenditure, can acquire and enjoy a collection of some of these delightful, charming or whimsical porcelain figural articles which the Germans have named nippes but which we usually refer to as dresser dolls.

Collection of Verna Ortwine
Photo by Norma Werner

How do we classify this 8½" bisque figure clad only in long grey painted hose and high heeled slippers, and a fine wig?

She is clearly marked, as shown, and we suspect her origin was France although we cannot be sure.

$200.00-250.00

Collection of Joyce Mineart

Figurines, statuettes, shelf pieces . . . whatever they're called, these small porcelain ornamental pieces were nearly as numerous as the more useful dresser dolls.

This young lady has the bobbed hair and kimono sleeves associated with the mid-1920's.

Besides the mark shown, she is stamped with the Limbach trademark of a crown and trefoil.

$50.00-100.00

Collection of Joyce Mineart

In the 1920's and early 30's almost every porcelain factory included in its catalog some models of figurines such as this young woman dancing with carefully studied abandonment. Her high heeled slippers match her green 2-piece costume.
　Incised "15218."

$50.00-100.00

Collection of Joyce Mineart

This colorful dragonfly lady is actually a vase with two compartments for small flowers.
　Unmarked

Up to $50.00

120

Collection of Norma Werner

A 7¼" wall vase of the type very popular in the 1920's, this was probably one of a pair of Spanish dancers.

It was made by Schneider and bears the appropriate trademark plus the incised "16071/GERMANY."

One of the many artifacts of the recent past which the Germans term "Nippes."

Up to $50.00

Collection of Joyce Mineart

A 2" novelty china head of a very distressed infant. There is no opening except for the slot used to attach the fly.

Stamped on the base, which has been filled with plaster, are the words "MADE IN GERMANY."

A paperweight, perhaps?

The Germans call such pieces 'Scherzfiguren."

$50.00-100.00

5028

Collection of Norma Werner

A figural flower vase.

This 10½" gentle maiden in a lavender frock, white gloves and gold locket, stands demurely in front of a flower vase which is modeled onto her skirt.

How charming she would look in the spring with fresh lilacs fanning around her shoulders!

Besides the numerals shown here, she is marked "GERMANY" in gold.

Up to $50.00

Collection of Vicki Halliday   Photo by Don Halliday

This thoroughly modern Millie was intended to do double duty on the dressing table. Once sewn onto a pincushion she will also guard hat pins thrust into the small container she leans against.

Up to $50.00

Collection of Norma Werner

Small pieces like this 3" young lady rising from her chair to curtsey carried out the popular Old-Fashioned Girl motif of the early 1920's.

We believe she was made by the Ernst Bohne Sohn factory in Rudolstadt.

Up to $50.00

Collection of Marie Burdick

W. Goebel Porzellanfabrik, Oeslau, West Germany, made and marked this novelty porcelain head. 3¾" high, glazed inside and out, this Flapper with her open mouth may have held sewing or dressing table items, or perhaps cigarettes.

$50.00-100.00

Collection of Norma Werner

    A handsome pair of gold trimmed china bookends, both incised "6687/Germany."
*Each figure holds a book, but whereas the gentleman's is open and he is reading print
in gold lines, the lady's is closed while she sits dreaming.*
    We wish we knew the titles of the novels that were held between them.

$100.00-150.00 pair

INDEX